**A Pillar Box Red Publication**

in association with

**THE BEST FOOTBALL MAGAZINE!**

ISBN: 978-1-912456-62-8

Photographs: © Getty Images.

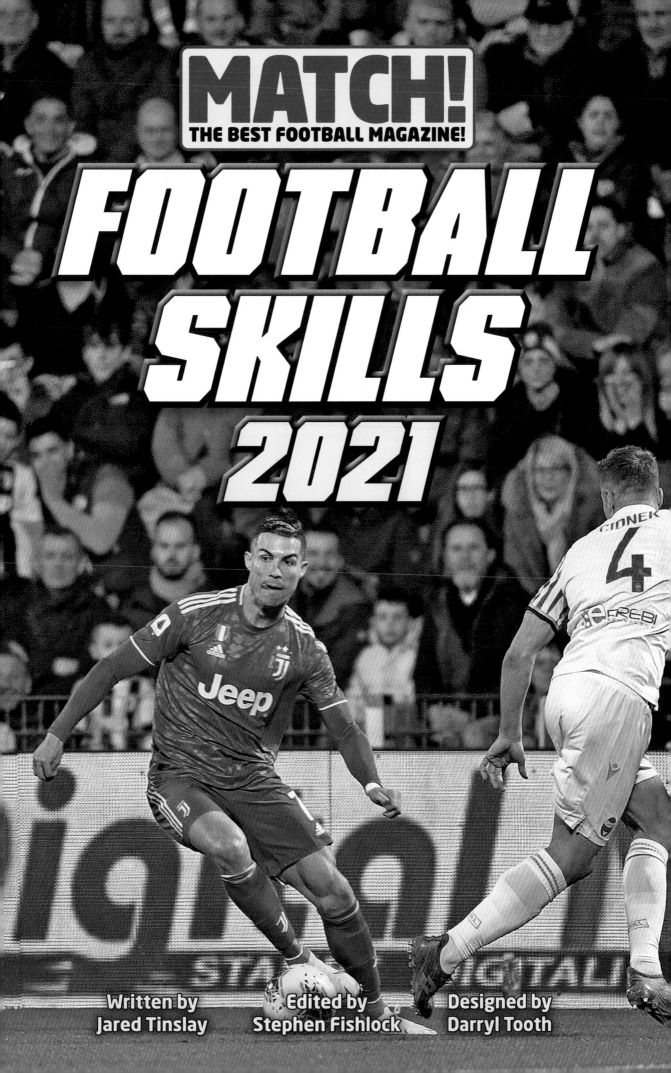

# MATCH!
## THE BEST FOOTBALL MAGAZINE!

# FOOTBALL SKILLS 2021

Written by
Jared Tinslay

Edited by
Stephen Fishlock

Designed by
Darryl Tooth

# CONTENTS

### THE COUNTDOWN BEGINS

**50 CALLUM HUDSON-ODOI**
Club: Chelsea
Country: England
DOB: 07/11/2000

**49 EMILIANO BUENDIA**
Club: Norwich
Country: Argentina
DOB: 25/12/1996

**47 BERNARD**
Club: Everton
Country: Brazil

**TOP SKILL! THE CRUYFF TURN!**

**48 GRADY DIANGANA**
Club: West Ham
Country: England
DOB: 19/04/1998

**TOP SKILL! THE DRAG TO DRAG!**

**46 LUCAS MOURA**
Club: Tottenham
Country: Brazil
DOB: 13/08/1992

**45 JOAO FELIX**
Club: Atletico Madrid
Country: Portugal
DOB: 10/11/1999

### F2 TEKKERS TIPS!

MATCH catches up with THE F2 heroes BILLY and JEZ to get some top-quality tips on how to become freestyle legends!

**PRACTISE ALONE OR WITH A MATE?**

**HOW MUCH PRACTICE?**

**STAYING MOTIVATED!**

**LEARN FROM THE BEST!**

**BUILDING CONFIDENCE!**

### QUIZ 1

**WORDFIT**
Fit the skillers that just missed out on this year's countdown into this massive grid!

Acosta
Alli
Bernardeschi
Bulasie
Chiesa
Corona
Draxler
Dybala
Eda
Giovinco
Grealish
Havit
Ibrahimovic
Insigne
James
Lo Celso
Maddison
Mane
Marlos
Martins
McGeady
Nani
Piatti
Quaresma
Saka
Sarr
Shapiri
Tadic
Talisca
Traore

NANI

**5 QUESTIONS ON... EDEN HAZARD**

1 Is the classy winger younger or older than his footy-playing brother Thorgan?

2 True or False? Eden has made over 100 appearances for his national side Belgium!

3 Name the French side he played at before joining Chelsea back in 2012?

4 Who did he score his last Chelsea goal against – in the 2019 Europa League final?

5 True or False? He had a poster of Zinedine Zidane on his bedroom wall as a child!

**SPOT THE BALL!**
Mark where you think the ball should be in this cool action shot!

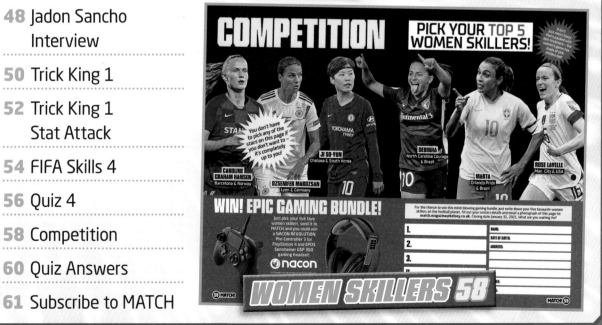

# 50

## CALLUM HUDSON-ODOI

**Club:** *Chelsea*
**Country:** *England*
**DOB:** *07/11/2000*

Blues supporters celebrated like mad when their awesome homegrown hero signed a new contract to keep him at the club until 2024, and so did MATCH - we get to watch him tear up the Premier League for at least another few seasons! He played loads of futsal growing up - and you can tell by the way the ball sticks to his feet like Super Glue!

| CONFIDENCE | DRIBBLING | TRICKS | AGILITY | WEAK FOOT |
|---|---|---|---|---|
| 78 | 82 | 77 | 84 | 76 |

# 49

## EMILIANO BUENDIA

**Club:** *Norwich*
**Country:** *Argentina*
**DOB:** *25/12/1996*

He was born on Christmas Day - and Buendia's been an epic present for English footy! He grew up in the same region as legendary Argentina dribbler Diego Maradona - and the silky skiller has the ability to go on similar mazy runs, plus the vision to open up defences. We can't believe he's never won a senior cap for his country!

| CONFIDENCE | DRIBBLING | TRICKS | AGILITY | WEAK FOOT |
|---|---|---|---|---|
| 82 | 80 | 81 | 81 | 84 |

# 48

## GRADY DIANGANA

**Club:** *West Ham*
**Country:** *England*
**DOB:** *19/04/1998*

We've seen the Young Lions attacking midfielder perform keepy-uppies with his head in an actual match - he puts the trick-performing seals at your local zoo to shame! With his proper low centre of gravity, bursts of pace and monster potential, we can see him being even higher up this tekkers list next year!

## TOP SKILL!
### THE DRAG TO DRAG!

| CONFIDENCE | DRIBBLING | TRICKS | AGILITY | WEAK FOOT |
|---|---|---|---|---|
| 85 | 79 | 84 | 80 | 76 |

# 47
## BERNARD

**Club:** *Everton*

**Country:** *Brazil*

**DOB:** *08/09/1992*

If you can't remember Bernard's stunning individual goal against West Ham from 2019-20, we recommend you watch it again... right now! The winger skins past two opponents, before poking the ball into the back of the net – and it's that uncanny ability to embarrass defenders that gets him into this year's top 50!

★ **TOP SKILL!** THE CRUYFF TURN!

| CONFIDENCE | DRIBBLING | TRICKS | AGILITY | WEAK FOOT |
|---|---|---|---|---|
| 86 | 80 | 83 | 80 | 77 |

# 46
## LUCAS MOURA

**Club:** *Tottenham*

**Country:** *Brazil*

**DOB:** *13/08/1992*

From one brilliant Brazilian to another... Lucas loves receiving the ball out wide and using his rapid speed to run directly at opponents! His feet are so quick that, even when defenders think they can nick the ball away, he sneaks another touch and forces them to either make a foul or let him pass!

# 45
## JOAO FELIX

**Club:** *Atletico Madrid*

**Country:** *Portugal*

**DOB:** *10/11/1999*

All the staff at Atletico Madrid's training ground have got to be really careful when they open Felix's personal locker – it's absolutely bursting with tricks! Can the 2019 Golden Boy winner follow in the footsteps of previous award winners like Lionel Messi and Paul Pogba to become a total trick king?

| CONFIDENCE | DRIBBLING | TRICKS | AGILITY | WEAK FOOT |
|---|---|---|---|---|
| 80 | 82 | 84 | 93 | 83 |

| CONFIDENCE | DRIBBLING | TRICKS | AGILITY | WEAK FOOT |
|---|---|---|---|---|
| 85 | 84 | 86 | 86 | 85 |

## 44
### RICHARLISON

**Club:** *Everton*
**Country:** *Brazil*
**DOB:** 10/05/1997

In MATCH's opinion, Richarlison's position on this list depends on his confidence levels! He's one of those players who can really struggle when he doesn't feel comfortable, or look like an absolute world-beater when he's flying – and then deserve to be ten spots higher instead!

| CONFIDENCE | DRIBBLING | TRICKS | AGILITY | WEAK FOOT |
|:---:|:---:|:---:|:---:|:---:|
| 77 | 88 | 85 | 82 | 75 |

## 43
### TANGUY NDOMBELE

**Club:** *Tottenham*
**Country:** *France*
**DOB:** 28/12/1996

You could put Ndombele in the middle of the hardest maze in the world and he'd still find his way out with the ball at his feet! His close control is so good that he can shimmy, spin and roulette his way out of some dangerous situations, while at the same time looking like he's barely bothered at all. The France CM's a top baller!

| CONFIDENCE | DRIBBLING | TRICKS | AGILITY | WEAK FOOT |
|:---:|:---:|:---:|:---:|:---:|
| 82 | 84 | 88 | 80 | 80 |

## 42
### STEPHAN EL SHAARAWY

**Club:** *Shanghai Shenhua*
**Country:** *Italy*
**DOB:** 27/10/1992

We reckon the ex-Roma wing wizard must be rolling in cash – not because he's earning big bucks in China, but because he totally sells defenders every game! He's definitely got the ability to be playing for a top European club, but he must love being his team's star man too much to return!

| CONFIDENCE | DRIBBLING | TRICKS | AGILITY | WEAK FOOT |
|:---:|:---:|:---:|:---:|:---:|
| 82 | 84 | 88 | 85 | 80 |

## 41
### SAID BENRAHMA

**Club:** *Brentford*
**Country:** *Algeria*
**DOB:** 10/08/1995

Playing Championship footy for Brentford since 2018 means skill king Benrahma has been out of the Premier League spotlight, but we were shocked he didn't have five-star skills on FIFA 20 – he was Rainbow Flicking his way past defenders in England's second tier! We can't wait to see even more of him in 2020-21!

| CONFIDENCE | DRIBBLING | TRICKS | AGILITY | WEAK FOOT |
|:---:|:---:|:---:|:---:|:---:|
| 85 | 80 | 90 | 84 | 80 |

# 40

## BERNARDO SILVA

**Club:** *Man. City*
**Country:** *Portugal*
**DOB:** *10/08/1994*

Man. City team-mate Benjamin Mendy calls him 'Bubble Gum' coz the ball always sticks to his feet! That got us thinking... but what flavour would he be? We've gone for 'Berry Twist', because the Portugal playmaker loves twisting and turning his way past defenders!

**TOP SKILL!**
**LA CROQUETA!**

CONFIDENCE
85

DRIBBLING
92

TRICKS
80

AGILITY
85

WEAK FOOT
90

# F2 TEKKERS

## PRACTISE ALONE OR WITH A MATE?

**BILLY SAYS:** "It depends on what type of person you are but, if you're self-driven and don't get bored too easily, you can practise on your own. Sometimes you need people there to spur and push you on, to compete with you and get the best out of you. We both practised alone growing up – that's how we learnt the best, but it really depends on the individual!"

## STAYING MOTIVATED!

**JEZ SAYS:** "Every successful sports person has the same problems and setbacks – Lionel Messi might get knocked out of the quarter-finals of the Champions League, but it doesn't make him any less of a good player. In life, things don't always go your way – setbacks aren't unique to you, it's just how you come back from them!"

**BILLY SAYS:** "Yeah, learn from your setbacks! That's what makes you better. As much as you learn from the good, you learn even more from the bad, and every single professional in the world has had to go through setbacks to get where they are now!"

## BUILDING CONFIDENCE!

**BILLY SAYS:** "I always say, don't go onto the pitch and force it, expecting to do ten or 20 skills – just have a skill that you're comfortable doing, or a favourite skill that you know works. Focus on using that skill, rather than thinking of ten different ones. Some skills come naturally to you, as well – when you overthink them, they don't really work! If I've got the ball on the wing, and a defender comes towards me, it's only then I think about what skill I'm going to use!"

# TIPS!

## HOW MUCH PRACTICE?

**BILLY SAYS:** "It's hard to say in hours, but what I will say is this – if you want to be the best at something, you have to practise as much as you possibly can. That doesn't mean not doing your homework, or helping out around the house – after doing all the other things you have to do, use that spare time to practise to give yourself the best chance to succeed. If you've done all of that and still don't succeed, at least you can say that you've given it a go!"

## LEARN FROM THE BEST!

**JEZ SAYS:** "Don't just think that those hours practising are all you need to improve your game. For example, if you're a left-back and want to improve that position, you could spend an hour and a half studying the best left-back in the world on a player cam, or turn the volume off on the TV and watch the game from a different perspective than a fan would. It's easy to watch football as a fan, but trying to analyse a player can really help your game!"

**BILLY SAYS:** "That's right. Even if it's not a form of physical practising – just watching a player can help you learn and develop your football skills!"

Photos by Dan Rouse.

# FIFA SKILLS

## BASICS
*Every decent FIFA player should know these basic skill moves!*

### SKILL MOVES GUIDE

Any arrows that are facing upward mean you should flick or hold the analogue stick in the direction your player is facing. Simple!

You can find out what your player's skill rating is by checking player info. The more stars they have, the more skilful they are!

You don't have to worry about learning every single trick all at once – mastering two or three is way more effective on FIFA!

---

### FAKE SHOT ★

This move looks best when you use it on the goalkeeper, so bust it out with a clinical striker – like the Uruguay legend!

**TAP:** Circle/B + Cross/A

PERFECT PLAYER
— LUIS SUAREZ

---

### SETUP TOUCH ★

This is good for lining up a strike from the edge of the box, so someone with a rocket shot like De Bruyne is ideal!

**HOLD:** R1/RB + **FLICK:** R Stick

PERFECT PLAYER
KEVIN DE BRUYNE

---

## DRAG BACK ★★

A drag back can give a midfielder an extra bit of time and space, so players with a quality passing range love it!

**HOLD:** R1/RB + L Stick Down

R1 / RB + L ↓

**1**

**2**

**PERFECT PLAYER**
**TONI KROOS**

## BALL ROLL ★★

Strikers with high dribbling stats like Firmino can use this move to buy a bit of space in the box before shooting!

**HOLD:** R Stick Left          **OR HOLD:** R Stick Right

R ←          R →

**PERFECT PLAYER**
**ROBERTO FIRMINO**

**1**

**2**

# 39

## GERARD DEULOFEU

**TOP SKILL!**
THE SHOULDER DROP!

CONFIDENCE
84

DRIBBLING
88

TRICKS
84

AGILITY
93

WEAK FOOT
85

**Club:** *Watford*
**Country:** *Spain*
**DOB:** 13/03/1994

Watford fans were devastated when Deulofeu suffered a bad knee injury towards the end of last season – they rely on him big time going forward! He was their most successful dribbler statistically the past two Prem seasons, and also created more chances in the last campaign than any other Hornets hero!

# 38
## SOFIANE BOUFAL

**Club:** *Southampton*
**Country:** *Morocco*
**DOB:** *17/09/1993*

He's nicknamed the 'Moroccan Magician' because he pulls tons of tricks out of the bag - just don't expect to see him revealing rabbits from his socks! As well as all the flash tricks, he's got one of the best first touches on the planet - if there was a ball control boost, he'd be even higher!

| CONFIDENCE | DRIBBLING | TRICKS | AGILITY | WEAK FOOT |
|---|---|---|---|---|
| 84 | 88 | 85 | 89 | 86 |

# 37
## MESUT OZIL

**Club:** *Arsenal*
**Country:** *Germany*
**DOB:** *15/10/1988*

Ozil's another star who thrives massively on confidence but, when he's on his game, there aren't many players that can match his swagger! He simply drifts around the pitch, knitting things together - and pulls off the odd crowd-pleasing nutmeg and backheel when the occasion presents itself. We want more!

| CONFIDENCE | DRIBBLING | TRICKS | AGILITY | WEAK FOOT |
|---|---|---|---|---|
| 80 | 85 | 87 | 88 | 88 |

## TOP SKILL!
### THE FLIP-FLAP!

# 36
## WILLIAN

**Club:** *Arsenal*
**Country:** *Brazil*
**DOB:** *09/08/1988*

We wouldn't be surprised to see Willian on a television dance contest in the future - his mega quick feet, shoulder drops and Elasticos would be enough to make him the champion! He's also got great rhythm - he can slow the pace down, before accelerating off into distance at speed!

| CONFIDENCE | DRIBBLING | TRICKS | AGILITY | WEAK FOOT |
|---|---|---|---|---|
| 85 | 88 | 85 | 87 | 85 |

# 35

## MARCELO

**Club:** *Real Madrid*
**Country:** *Brazil*
**DOB:** *12/05/1988*

A mega MATCH shout-out to Marcelo for being the only defender on this countdown – and the only defender on recent FIFA editions to have five-star skills! Even though he's coming towards the end of his Real career, he hasn't lost his fine first touch or desire to drive forward!

| CONFIDENCE | DRIBBLING | TRICKS | AGILITY | WEAK FOOT |
|:---:|:---:|:---:|:---:|:---:|
| 87 | 88 | 88 | 85 | 86 |

# 34

## MOHAMED SALAH

**Club:** *Liverpool*
**Country:** *Egypt*
**DOB:** *15/06/1992*

As well as having some sick selfie skills, Mo's also a proper Prem megastar! His missing right foot is basically made up for by his incredible confidence and dribbling tekkers – and when you add to that all his goals and assists, The Reds have got themselves some player!

| CONFIDENCE | DRIBBLING | TRICKS | AGILITY | WEAK FOOT |
|:---:|:---:|:---:|:---:|:---:|
| 94 | 92 | 87 | 91 | 75 |

# 33

## DIMITRI PAYET

**Club:** *Marseille*
**Country:** *France*
**DOB:** *29/03/1987*

As top tekkers go, one of MATCH's favourite things to see is watching a player place the ball into the top bins from a set-piece – and Payet's one of the best at it! On top of his dead-ball deliveries, he's also able to weave his way past defenders using both feet, which not all players can do!

## TOP SKILL!
### THE FORWARD ROLL!

| CONFIDENCE | DRIBBLING | TRICKS | AGILITY | WEAK FOOT |
|:---:|:---:|:---:|:---:|:---:|
| 83 | 90 | 86 | 78 | 89 |

# 32
## ISCO

**Club:** *Real Madrid*
**Country:** *Spain*
**DOB:** 21/04/1992

Isco definitely isn't going to be the next 100m world champion, but there aren't many stars who have quicker feet then the silky Spain playmaker! He slaloms past his opponents at total ease, but what we really love about the Real star is his work rate – he'll bust a gut to win the ball back if he ever loses it!

| CONFIDENCE | DRIBBLING | TRICKS | AGILITY | WEAK FOOT |
|---|---|---|---|---|
| 90 | 92 | 88 | 86 | 93 |

# 31
## MARTIN ODEGAARD

**Club:** *Real Madrid*
**Country:** *Norway*
**DOB:** 17/12/1998

The Norway young gun's loan spell at Madrid's La Liga rivals Real Sociedad worked wonders for his confidence! As well as getting regular footy, Martin was also their star man, so they relied on him big time for creativity – it's just a shame Odegaard doesn't have much of a right foot!

| CONFIDENCE | DRIBBLING | TRICKS | AGILITY | WEAK FOOT |
|---|---|---|---|---|
| 93 | 90 | 94 | 85 | 70 |

# 30
## LEROY SANE

**Club:** *Bayern Munich*
**Country:** *Germany*
**DOB:** 11/01/1996

Even though he barely played any football in 2019-20, the German still sneaks into the top 30 of this countdown! His electrifying pace lets him burn away from defenders, while his body swerves and drag backs mean he can manoeuvre his way through packed backlines!

| CONFIDENCE | DRIBBLING | TRICKS | AGILITY | WEAK FOOT |
|---|---|---|---|---|
| 80 | 96 | 85 | 93 | 77 |

# WORDFIT

Fit the skillers that just missed out on this year's countdown into this massive grid!

| | | |
|---|---|---|
| Acosta | Grealish | McGeady |
| Alli | Harit | Nani |
| Bernardeschi | Ibrahimovic | Piatti |
| Bolasie | Insigne | Quaresma |
| Chiesa | James | Saka |
| Corona | Lo Celso | Sarr |
| Draxler | Maddison | Shaqiri |
| Dybala | Mane | Tadic |
| Elia | Marlos | Talisca |
| Giovinco | Martins | Traore |

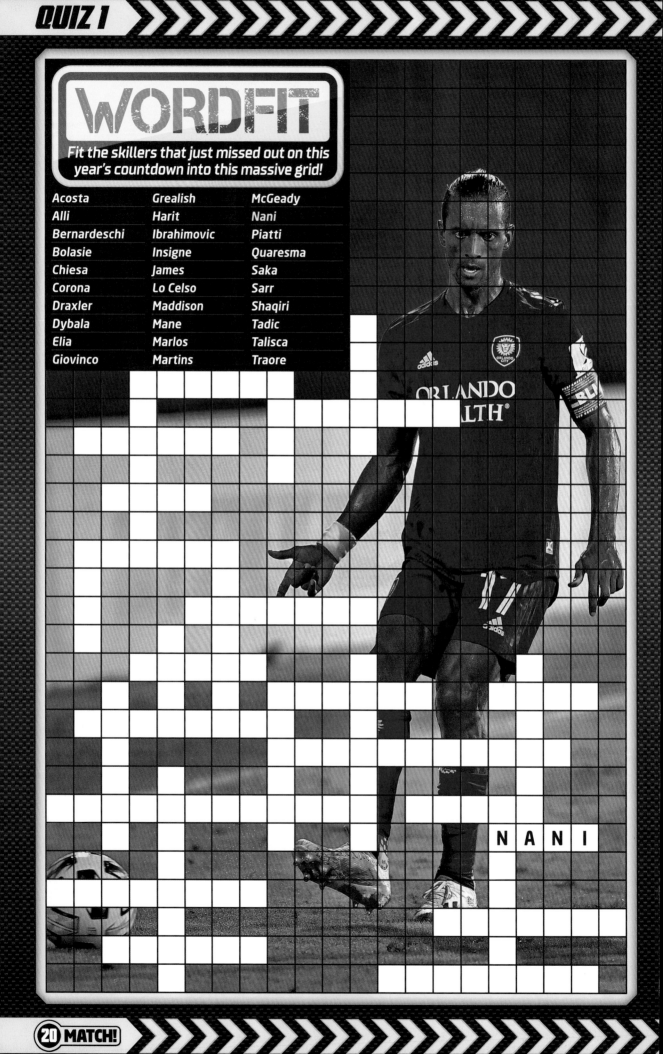

N A N I

# 5 QUESTIONS ON... EDEN HAZARD

1 Is the classy winger younger or older than his footy-playing brother Thorgan?

2 True or False? Eden has made over 100 appearances for his national side Belgium!

3 Name the French side he played at before joining Chelsea back in 2012!

4 Who did he score his last Chelsea goal against - in the 2019 Europa League final?

5 True or False? He had a poster of Zinedine Zidane on his bedroom wall as a child!

# SPOT THE BALL!

Mark where you think the ball should be in this cool action shot!

ANSWERS ON P6

# FIFA SKILLS

## HEEL FLICK ★★★

Rapid players like Mbappe can be deadly using this move, because it helps them to properly burst past defenders!

**FLICK:** R Stick Up | **THEN FLICK:** R Stick Down

**PERFECT PLAYER**
**KYLIAN MBAPPE**

## HEEL CHOP ★★★

Any rapid winger can use a heel chop to quickly change direction, but Cristiano Ronaldo is the master of it!

**HOLD:** L2/LT + fake shot (see page 14)

L2 / LT + ○ / B + X / A

**PERFECT PLAYER**
**CRISTIANO RONALDO**

## LATERAL HEEL TO HEEL ★★★

This move is the newer, smoother version of the heel chop, and world-class dribblers like Sancho are lethal with it!

**HOLD:** L1/LB — L1 / LB
**FLICK:** R Stick Right then Left — R → R ←

**PERFECT PLAYER**
**JADON SANCHO**

## DRAG TO DRAG ★★★★

You can use this move to set up a shooting opportunity. It's perfect for Depay – he's got tons of skill and a rocket shot!

**HOLD:** L2/LT + fake shot (see page 14) + Release L stick — L2 / LT + ○ / B + X / A

**PERFECT PLAYER**
**MEMPHIS DEPAY**

## 29
### QUINCY PROMES

**Club:** *Ajax*
**Country:** *Netherlands*
**DOB:** *04/01/1992*

The rapid forward was released by Ajax as a 16-year-old, but found his way back to the club in 2019 – 11 years later! He obviously felt he had a point to prove on his return, because he's totally torn it up for the Eredivisie giants – he scored 12 goals in 20 appearances in 2019-20, and has rinsed loads of defenders!

| CONFIDENCE | DRIBBLING | TRICKS | AGILITY | WEAK FOOT |
|:---:|:---:|:---:|:---:|:---:|
| 92 | 84 | 93 | 85 | 91 |

## 28
### PHILIPPE COUTINHO

**Club:** *Barcelona*
**Country:** *Brazil*
**DOB:** *12/06/1992*

Coutinho is so good at nutmegs, MATCH has even seen him 'meg' an ant! Okay... so it was a Nike advert, which MAY have had some visual effects, but the Brazil baller's still dangerously good at flicking the ball through his opponents' legs!

| CONFIDENCE | DRIBBLING | TRICKS | AGILITY | WEAK FOOT |
|:---:|:---:|:---:|:---:|:---:|
| 84 | 90 | 88 | 92 | 90 |

## 27
### NABIL FEKIR

**Club:** *Real Betis*
**Country:** *France*
**DOB:** *18/07/1993*

If you were to look up the footy definition of 'game changer', you'd probably find Fekir's name! He's the sort of star that can look totally uninterested, but it's just one of his tricks to fool opponents into a false sense of security – he knows that when the ball comes his way, he can make something happen at once!

| CONFIDENCE | DRIBBLING | TRICKS | AGILITY | WEAK FOOT |
|:---:|:---:|:---:|:---:|:---:|
| 84 | 90 | 88 | 92 | 90 |

### ★ TOP SKILL!
**THE TOE POKE PANNA!**

# 26
## MARCUS RASHFORD

**TOP SKILL!**
THE ELASTICO!

**Club:** *Man. United*
**Country:** *England*
**DOB:** *31/10/1997*

One of Rashford's most effective skill moves is literally just a simple drop of the shoulder, and then a burst of acceleration to drive away from defenders. He has some top tekkers too, though – it was his jaw-dropping Elastico against Brighton in the 2019-20 season that really had MATCH drooling. He nutmegged the defender with the skill, too!

| CONFIDENCE | DRIBBLING | TRICKS | AGILITY | WEAK FOOT |
|:---:|:---:|:---:|:---:|:---:|
| 88 | 86 | 94 | 89 | 78 |

---

# 25
## MEMPHIS DEPAY

**Club:** *Lyon*
**Country:** *Netherlands*
**DOB:** *13/02/1994*

Memphis loves to rap and write music in his spare time, and he brings that flow to the footy field with his slick stepovers, bamboozling body feints and sharp spins! Maybe he can take inspiration from making MATCH's top 25 trick machines for his next song?

| CONFIDENCE | DRIBBLING | TRICKS | AGILITY | WEAK FOOT |
|:---:|:---:|:---:|:---:|:---:|
| 90 | 84 | 94 | 85 | 80 |

---

# 24
## ANGEL DI MARIA

**Club:** *PSG*
**Country:** *Argentina*
**DOB:** *14/02/1988*

Forget the box of chocolates and super cheesy cards, the planet's best Valentine's Day present to football fans was Angel Di Maria – he really knows how to make defenders blush! He was born in the same city as Leo Messi, so there must be something in the air that produces demon dribblers!

| CONFIDENCE | DRIBBLING | TRICKS | AGILITY | WEAK FOOT |
|:---:|:---:|:---:|:---:|:---:|
| 89 | 87 | 92 | 86 | 88 |

# 23
## JUAN CUADRADO

**Club:** *Juventus*
**Country:** *Colombia*
**DOB:** *26/05/1988*

Here's a huge life lesson, readers... it's never too late to learn a new skill – just ask Juan! After injuries to a few Juve stars last season, the veteran winger was asked to play as a full-back – and he absolutely smashed it! He was able to get on the ball deeper and start his weavy runs even earlier!

| CONFIDENCE | DRIBBLING | TRICKS | AGILITY | WEAK FOOT |
|:---:|:---:|:---:|:---:|:---:|
| 90 | 90 | 90 | 91 | 78 |

# 22
## THIAGO ALCANTARA

**Club:** *Bayern Munich*
**Country:** *Spain*
**DOB:** *11/04/1991*

Thiago's a former Barcelona boy who came through their prestigious La Masia academy and won eight trophies at La Blaugrana! But one of the tricks he pulls off the best is actually The Roulette – made famous by legendary Real Madrid playmaker and manager Zinedine Zidane!

| CONFIDENCE | DRIBBLING | TRICKS | AGILITY | WEAK FOOT |
|:---:|:---:|:---:|:---:|:---:|
| 86 | 90 | 90 | 91 | 84 |

# 21
## ANTHONY MARTIAL

**Club:** *Man. United*
**Country:** *France*
**DOB:** *05/12/1995*

Martial had a trial at Man. City as a kid, but now he's bossing it for their city rivals! Ever since he burst onto the scene as a wonderkid for Monaco, he's been compared to Premier League legend Thierry Henry – the former France forward also played for the Ligue 1 club, and had similar pace and dribbling!

## ★ TOP SKILL!
### THE DRAG TO DRAG!

| CONFIDENCE | DRIBBLING | TRICKS | AGILITY | WEAK FOOT |
|:---:|:---:|:---:|:---:|:---:|
| 90 | 90 | 92 | 88 | 85 |

# 20
## ROBERTO FIRMINO

**Club:** *Liverpool*
**Country:** *Brazil*
**DOB:** *02/10/1991*

Even though he's currently Liverpool's main striker, we can see Bobby moving into a more creative midfield role in the future – like Wayne Rooney did! He's got the same creativity, vision and intelligence to pick defences apart, but also the knowledge of when to get into the box to finish off chances!

CONFIDENCE
90

DRIBBLING
88

TRICKS
93

AGILITY
81

WEAK FOOT
88

# LIV COO

## ...FREESTYLE STAR!

MATCH catches up with LIV COOKE, one member of the UEFA EURO 2020 mascot team, to chat about her epic freestyling career!

## HER JOURNEY!

**LIV SAYS:** "I've always been football crazy! I learnt to juggle sitting down after suffering a bad back injury playing for Blackburn's academy. It wasn't long until I discovered the world of freestyle football and fell in love with it. I carried on learning freestyle football while still trying to play football for a year, but I then realised I couldn't be the best freestyler in the world AND play footy for England, so I had to choose!"

## TRAINING HARD!

**LIV SAYS:** "When I first started I didn't even realise I was training. I was in my garden pretty much all day every day trying to land new tricks. At 15, when I decided I wanted to be the best in the world, I was training around six to eight hours a day, six days a week! This was as well as taking notes, analysing my moves and working on my mindset for a few hours a day."

## BEING A FREESTYLER!

**LIV SAYS:** "I'm living my dream! Actually, it's beyond anything I'd ever dreamed of! I'm still working every day and chasing progress – I trust in hard work. It's also so rewarding to see how other people can be inspired to take up freestyling or just have more confidence in what they do!"

## FAVOURITE MOMENT!

**LIV SAYS:** "Of course, achieving my dream of becoming world champion is, and probably always will be, my favourite moment, but there are other big ones - like the honour of being selected as a UEFA EURO 2020 freestyler. Being able to take the beauty of freestyling, street football and panna to football fans all over Europe is a really special opportunity!"

## FAVOURITE TRICK!

**LIV SAYS:** "My signature move is now the 'thigh pop', which is when the ball is trapped between your heel and bum. When you extend your leg sharply, you pop the ball out and upwards. I have lots of variations of this trick, like popping the ball up during a roly poly, during a handstand or even an around the world!"

## STAYING MOTIVATED!

**LIV SAYS:** "I probably find myself getting frustrated and not being able to do a trick more often than people expect. It happens, especially when you're trying to push yourself and learn new things. I just try to keep my mind in a positive state, so I'll put songs on that do exactly that!"

## TOP ADVICE!

**LIV SAYS:** "Sometimes when I meet kids they say things along the lines of 'I want to be like you when I grow up.' This is so lovely to hear, but it also frustrates me because I want them to raise the bar. I tell them 'No! You must aim higher than that - you can be way better than me! You can achieve anything you want if you put your mind to it. Promise me you'll aim higher than me!'"

# CROSSWORD

Use the clues to fill in MATCH's tricky crossword puzzle!

## ACROSS

2. Shirt number that Roberto Firmino wears for Liverpool! (4)

5. Prem team Marseille signed Dimitri Payet from in 2017! (4,3)

7. Number of league titles Paul Pogba won at Juventus! (4)

10. Foot Leroy Sane prefers to use! (4)

11. English city Chelsea wonderkid Callum Hudson-Odoi grew up in! (6)

12. Number of league goals Marcus Rashford scored in 2018-19! (8)

14. Sick boot brand baller Bernardo Silva wears! (6)

16. Lionel Messi's weird 'La Pulga' nickname in English! (3,4)

18. Country where Nicolas Pepe was born! (6)

19. African country winger Samuel Chukwueze represents! (7)

## DOWN

1. Position Brazil baller Marcelo normally plays! (4,4)

3. Country Jadon Sancho scored his first England goals against! (6)

4. German club Barcelona signed Ousmane Dembele from back in 2017! (8,8)

6. Spanish team Emiliano Buendia spent some of his youth career with (4,6)

8. La Liga side Martin Odegaard spent 2019-20 on loan at! (4,8)

9. Boot brand Lyon skiller Memphis Depay wears! (5,6)

13. Month Brazil wonderkid Rodrygo was born! (7)

15. Name of Thiago's younger brother who's played for Barcelona, Celta Vigo and Inter! (7)

16. Number of countries Quincy Promes has played professional footy in! (5)

17. Shirt number Kylian Mbappe usually wears for France! (3)

# THE NICKNAME GAME

Have a go at matching the world-class trick machines to their awesome nicknames!

| Douglas Costa | Kingsley Coman | Jadon Sancho | Philippe Coutinho | Stephan El Shaarawy | Marcus Rashford |
|---|---|---|---|---|---|
| 1 | 2 | 3 | 4 | 5 | 6 |

| A | B | C | D | E | F |
|---|---|---|---|---|---|
| Flash | The Pharaoh | The Little Magician | The King | The Rocket | Beansprouts |

## ODD ONE OUT!

Nicolas Pepe

Nabil Fekir

Bernardo Silva

Marcelo

Allan Saint-Maximin

Which of these top-quality dribblers has NEVER played in France's Ligue 1?

Anthony Martial

# TOP SKILL!
## THE ROULETTE!

19

**PAUL POGBA**

CONFIDENCE
88

DRIBBLING
84

TRICKS
92

AGILITY
80

WEAK FOOT
93

**Club:** *Man. United*
**Country:** *France*
**DOB:** *15/03/1993*

He might need 13 little steps to take a penalty, but all it takes is one big swoop over the ball to completely fool an onrushing defender! Injuries might have set him back slightly over the past two seasons, but he's still one of the brainiest ballers on the planet - he can tell you how to say 'nutmeg' in four different languages, after all. LOL!

# 18

## OUSMANE DEMBELE

**Club:** *Barcelona*
**Country:** *France*
**DOB:** *15/05/1997*

Just like Pogba, the Barcelona speedster has suffered tons of injuries - he hasn't made more than 22 starts in any season of his career so far! We've still seen more than enough to include him in our top 20, though - his dribble cuts sit defenders on their bums, and then he uses his long legs to stride past them at speed!

**TOP SKILL!**
**THE DRIBBLE CUT!**

| CONFIDENCE | DRIBBLING | TRICKS | AGILITY | WEAK FOOT |
|:---:|:---:|:---:|:---:|:---:|
| 88 | 84 | 92 | 80 | 93 |

---

# 17

## SAMUEL CHUKWUEZE

**Club:** *Villarreal*
**Country:** *Nigeria*
**DOB:** *22/05/1999*

Chukwueze is a non-mover from last year's countdown! He's actually got a really similar playing style to Dembele - he's a left-footed winger, who plays from the right wing, and loves cutting in on his stronger foot to get shots away. He could move further up the list next year!

| CONFIDENCE | DRIBBLING | TRICKS | AGILITY | WEAK FOOT |
|:---:|:---:|:---:|:---:|:---:|
| 89 | 85 | 91 | 91 | 76 |

---

# 16

## DAVID NERES

**Club:** *Ajax*
**Country:** *Brazil*
**DOB:** *03/03/1997*

The problem with trying to mark Neres is, even if he doesn't skin you with one of his sideway swerves or eye-popping stepovers, he'll just knock the ball past you and beat you for pace instead! Even if you give him a few extra yards, he'll still find a way to get past you!

| CONFIDENCE | DRIBBLING | TRICKS | AGILITY | WEAK FOOT |
|:---:|:---:|:---:|:---:|:---:|
| 89 | 85 | 91 | 91 | 76 |

## 15
### RODRYGO

**Club:** *Real Madrid*
**Country:** *Brazil*
**DOB:** 09/01/2001

The Samba sensation is nicknamed the 'Next Neymar' in his home country – and it's easy to see the comparisons! As well as coming through the same academy, and eventually donning the same No.11 jersey for Santos, he also shares the same desire to get the crowd on their feet!

| CONFIDENCE | DRIBBLING | TRICKS | AGILITY | WEAK FOOT |
|:---:|:---:|:---:|:---:|:---:|
| 95 | 93 | 93 | 86 | 78 |

---

## 14
### DOUGLAS COSTA

**Club:** *Juventus*
**Country:** *Brazil*
**DOB:** 14/09/1990

MATCH has actually seen Costa receive the ball in his own penalty box and, instead of playing a simple ball back to the keeper to clear, decide to take on the player pressing him until the opponent eventually fell onto his backside! That epic dribbling ability should come with a 'don't try this at home' warning. Wow!

| CONFIDENCE | DRIBBLING | TRICKS | AGILITY | WEAK FOOT |
|:---:|:---:|:---:|:---:|:---:|
| 89 | 92 | 95 | 93 | 79 |

---

## 13
### NICOLAS PEPE

**Club:** *Arsenal*
**Country:** *Ivory Coast*
**DOB:** 29/05/1995

The Gunners apparently only had £40 million to spend in the summer transfer window of 2019, so they must have been hugely impressed by Pepe to splash out a record £72 million on him! He had a sick first season in the Prem, showing off his quick feet and completing more dribbles than any other team-mate!

| CONFIDENCE | DRIBBLING | TRICKS | AGILITY | WEAK FOOT |
|:---:|:---:|:---:|:---:|:---:|
| 94 | 93 | 90 | 92 | 75 |

## 12
### ALLAN
### SAINT-MAXIMIN

**Club:** Newcastle
**Country:** France
**DOB:** 12/03/1997

In his last season at Nice before moving to the Prem, he completed more Ligue 1 dribbles than any other player - including Kylian Mbappe, Neymar and Nicolas Pepe! Let's face it, when you spend £180 on a Gucci headband, you're probably gonna be pretty flash on the footy field too!

| CONFIDENCE | DRIBBLING | TRICKS | AGILITY | WEAK FOOT |
|:---:|:---:|:---:|:---:|:---:|
| 93 | 90 | 95 | 93 | 87 |

## 11
### KINGSLEY
### COMAN

**Club:** Bayern Munich
**Country:** France
**DOB:** 13/06/1996

Season after season, Coman seems to suffer a nightmare injury, and that's got to knock his confidence - but he can take a big morale boost from the fact MATCH has boosted him up one spot from last year's countdown! Why? He's still the Stepover King and a Cruyff-Turn specialist!

| CONFIDENCE | DRIBBLING | TRICKS | AGILITY | WEAK FOOT |
|:---:|:---:|:---:|:---:|:---:|
| 85 | 92 | 95 | 92 | 90 |

## TOP SKILL!
### THE REVERSE DRAG PUSH!

## 10
### LIONEL
### MESSI

**Club:** Barcelona
**Country:** Argentina
**DOB:** 24/06/1987

The 2019-20 Champions League's most successful dribbler is ridiculously hard to get the ball off - he doesn't need to showboat when he can simply use his low centre of gravity, agility and quick feet to run rings around defenders! His decision-making is also epic - and that's what makes a great footballer a world megastar!

| CONFIDENCE | DRIBBLING | TRICKS | AGILITY | WEAK FOOT |
|:---:|:---:|:---:|:---:|:---:|
| 99 | 95 | 85 | 93 | 85 |

# FIFA SKILLS

## DEADLY DRIBBLING

These top moves will tie defenders in knots!

### ROULETTE ★★★

Zizou loved the roulette as it combines his big strengths - unreal tekkers, while using strength to protect the ball!

**ROTATE:** R Stick 270°    **OR ROTATE:** R Stick 270°

R ↓ ← ↑ →    R ↓ → ↑ ←

**PERFECT PLAYER**
**ZINEDINE ZIDANE**

1

2

### LANE CHANGE ★★★★

Also known as 'La Croqueta', this move was added to FIFA as a tribute to Barcelona and Spain legend Andres Iniesta!

**HOLD:** L1/LB + R Stick Left    **OR HOLD:** L1/LB + R Stick Right

L1 / LB + R ←    L1 / LB + R →

**PERFECT PLAYER**
**ANDRES INIESTA**

1

2

## STOP AND TURN ★★★★

Kai Havertz can use his long legs and epic strength to block defenders from getting a glimpse of the ball!

**FLICK:** R Stick Up then R Stick Left

**OR:** R Stick Up then R Stick Right

R ↑ R ←     R ↑ R →

**PERFECT PLAYER**
**KAI HAVERTZ**

**1**

**2**

## DRAG BACK SPIN ★★★★

Players with high agility like Coutinho are perfect for this move because they can change direction so quickly!

**FLICK:** R Stick Down then R Stick Left

**OR:** R Stick Down then R Stick Right

R ↓ R ←     R ↓ R →

**PERFECT PLAYER**
**PHILIPPE COUTINHO**

**1**

**2**

# KNUCKLEBALL!

## THE RUN-UP...

"The run-up should consist of five to seven steps directly back from the ball, with two steps either side, depending on what foot you strike the ball with. Your stance should be at a slight angle, approach the ball on your toes at a steady pace, with the last stride the biggest. This enables your kicking foot to open up and make the correct contact!"

## WHAT'S A KNUCKLEBALL?

"A knuckleball is a shot where the ball swerves and dips with little or no rotation!"

## THE CONTACT AREA...

"For the contact, you want to be striking the ball with the 'instep' part of your foot – aka 'the sweet spot'. You're gonna need to open up your striking foot 90 degrees, as if you are performing a side-foot pass, to make contact with your instep. This is the hardest bone in your foot, and is vital in order to perfect the knuckleball technique!"

## STRIKING THE BALL...

"When making contact, it's important to strike the centre of the ball – if you don't strike the ball in the centre, the ball will have back spin or curve on it, resulting in no knuckleball effect. When you place the ball for a free-kick, make sure you have a logo or ball marking facing you as you approach it. This will help you strike the ball in the centre. The valve can also be a good point of reference!"

## DIFFICULTY RATING!

"8/10"

Wicked YouTube superstars THE KNUCKLEBALL TWINS give MATCH a step-by-step guide on how to strike the sweetest knuckleball free-kick around!

# WICKED VIDEOS!

Here are five of our favourite KNUCKLEBALL TWINS videos from their YouTube channel!

## FOLLOW THROUGH...

"As you make contact with the ball, put your weight on your left shoulder and lean your body to the left, with your head over the ball - or the reverse for left footers. The follow through must be short and snappy, to ensure there's little rotation on the ball after contact. As you start to practise, shoot from a short distance to allow your technique to adapt from a curve shot to a knuckleball!"

### TOP TIP!

"It will take time to learn, so be patient and try to find a method that suits you - don't be scared to adjust different parts of the technique to suit your ability!"

### WHO TO WATCH?

"Cristiano Ronaldo!"

## WHERE TO AIM...

"The knuckleball is the most unpredictable shot out there, so in terms of aiming a free-kick, this is what makes it so exciting! You could be aiming for the middle of the goal, and the movement of the ball could make it fly into the top corner! We normally aim our free-kicks high into the corners, as it gives the knuckleball shot the best chance to be the most effective. A low knuckleball towards the goal can be effective, providing the distance isn't too far!"

**1** The guys test out which boots work best for a knuckleball free-kick!

**2** Sammy sees how many attempts he needs to hit the perfect FK past Charlie!

**3** Sammy tries to score a knuckleball from a crazy angle!

**4** Watch the free-kicks from a really cool view – the camera in top bins!

**5** The guys imagine taking FKs against a seven-foot defensive wall!

Watch the videos on their YouTube channel, and then follow them on social media @knuckleballtwins

# 9

## EDEN HAZARD

**TOP SKILL!**
**CUT AND TURN!**

**Club:** *Real Madrid*
**Country:** *Belgium*
**DOB:** *07/01/1991*

Around 50,000 supporters flocked to the Bernabeu in the summer of 2019 – not to watch a pre-season friendly, but the official unveiling of the Belgium megastar as a Real Madrid player! He left the Premier League as the best dribbler and top assister, but an injury-plagued first season in Spain sees him stay in ninth place on this list!

**CONFIDENCE**
**95**

**DRIBBLING**
**97**

**TRICKS**
**88**

**AGILITY**
**95**

**WEAK FOOT**
**90**

## TOP SKILL!
### THE BODY FEINT!

## 8
## HAKIM ZIYECH

**Club:** *Chelsea*
**Country:** *Morocco*
**DOB:** *19/03/1993*

We couldn't believe it took so long for a club in Europe's top five leagues to snap up Ziyech - he'd been wowing the Eredivisie for years before Chelsea landed him! Since making his Ajax debut back in 2016, up until the point of The Blues announcing his deal, the star had created more chances and been involved in more goals than anyone in the league!

| CONFIDENCE | DRIBBLING | TRICKS | AGILITY | WEAK FOOT |
|---|---|---|---|---|
| 95 | 92 | 93 | 92 | 80 |

## 7
## CRISTIANO RONALDO

**Club:** *Juventus*
**Country:** *Portugal*
**DOB:** *05/02/1985*

When Cristiano first emerged as a wicked wonderkid, MATCH used to get neck cramps from counting how many stepovers he could do in a game - but nowadays he's all about busting as many nets as possible! He's still a skiller deep down inside, though - he'll whip out his world-famous Ronaldo chop whenever the moment presents itself!

## TOP SKILL!
### THE STEPOVER CHOP!

| CONFIDENCE | DRIBBLING | TRICKS | AGILITY | WEAK FOOT |
|---|---|---|---|---|
| 98 | 89 | 95 | 87 | 94 |

# 6

## VINICIUS JUNIOR

**Club:** *Real Madrid*
**Country:** *Brazil*
**DOB:** *12/07/2000*

Vinicius receives a load of stick from some fans over his finishing, but we reckon they need to give the kid a break! He's only just starting his career, and has already established himself as one of the most outrageous skillers on the planet - he's got plenty of time to add goals to his game!

**TOP SKILL!**
THE OUTSIDE SCOOP!

| CONFIDENCE | DRIBBLING | TRICKS | AGILITY | WEAK FOOT |
|---|---|---|---|---|
| 96 | 95 | 96 | 97 | 85 |

---

# 5

## KYLIAN MBAPPE

**TOP SKILL!**
THE FAKE RABONA!

**Club:** *PSG*
**Country:** *France*
**DOB:** *20/12/1998*

One youngster who's already developed all aspects of his game is World Cup winner Mbappe - he proved it by scoring one of MATCH's favourite goals of 2019-20 against Lyon! He cut out a ball in his own half, sprinted the length of the pitch - producing a stepover and fake shot to skin two defenders - and then busted the net at the end!

| CONFIDENCE | DRIBBLING | TRICKS | AGILITY | WEAK FOOT |
|---|---|---|---|---|
| 98 | 95 | 93 | 95 | 88 |

# 4

## RIYAD
## MAHREZ

**TOP SKILL!**
**THE STOP AND GO!**

**DID YOU KNOW?**
IN 2019-20, MAHREZ BECAME THE FIRST ALGERIAN TO SCORE 50 PREMIER LEAGUE GOALS. LEGEND!

**Club: Man. City**
**Country: Algeria**
**DOB: 21/02/1991**

You could blindfold Mahrez, smash a ball into the sky and he'd still be able to bring it down perfectly into his feet - his ball control is that good! And sometimes, he only actually needs his first touch to get past his man - he's the master of the disguise trap turn and disguise first touch!

**CONFIDENCE**
**96**

**DRIBBLING**
**95**

**TRICKS**
**95**

**AGILITY**
**95**

**WEAK FOOT**
**91**

## BRAIN-BUSTER!

How well do you know some of footy's best tricksters?

1. True or False? Real Madrid signed Rodrygo from the same Brazilian club that they signed Vinicius Jr!

2. Which English team did legendary skiller Jay-Jay Okocha not play for – Hull, Chelsea or Bolton?

3. Which English side did Everton sign silky Brazil baller Richarlison from in 2018?

4. How many Prem games did Philippe Coutinho play for Liverpool – more or less than 150?

5. Which Spanish side did Gerard Deulofeu start his career with – Barcelona, Sevilla or Valencia?

6. Which African country does Man. City winger Riyad Mahrez represent – Morocco or Algeria?

7. How old was Kylian Mbappe when he made his Ligue 1 debut for French giants Monaco in 2015?

8. Who was Willian's football idol when he was growing up – Ronaldinho or Thierry Henry?

9. How much did Tottenham pay to sign Tanguy Ndombele from Lyon – more or less than £50 million?

10. Name the awesome boot brand that Liverpool and Egypt legend Mohamed Salah loves to wear!

1.............................................
2.............................................
3.............................................
4.............................................
5.............................................
6.............................................
7.............................................
8.............................................
9.............................................
10...........................................

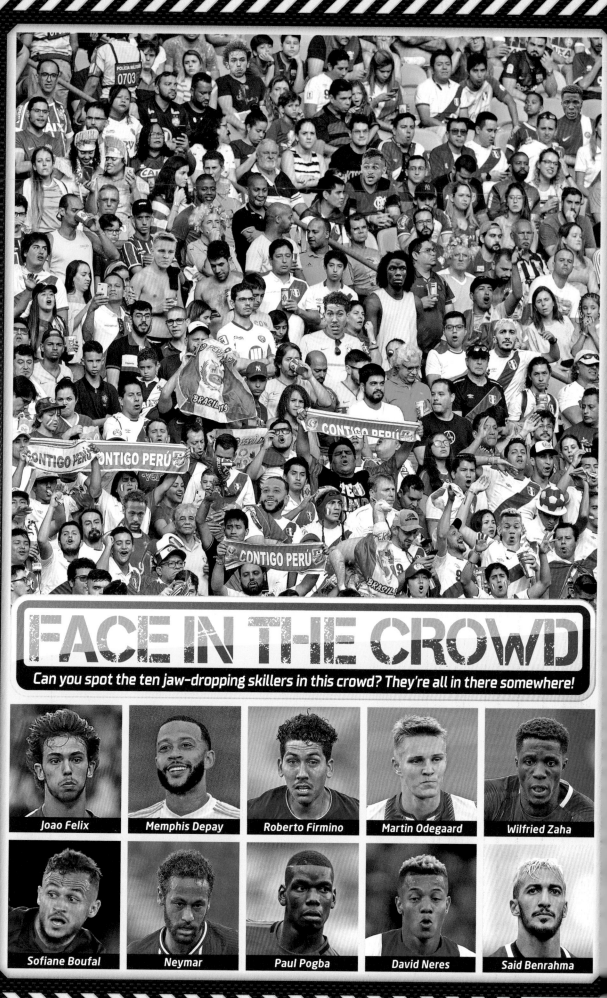

# FACE IN THE CROWD

Can you spot the ten jaw-dropping skillers in this crowd? They're all in there somewhere!

| Joao Felix | Memphis Depay | Roberto Firmino | Martin Odegaard | Wilfried Zaha |
| Sofiane Boufal | Neymar | Paul Pogba | David Neres | Said Benrahma |

ANSWER ON PAGE

# 3

## WILFRIED ZAHA

**TOP SKILL!**
THE HOCUS POCUS!

CONFIDENCE
**97**

DRIBBLING
**96**

TRICKS
**98**

AGILITY
**94**

WEAK FOOT
**84**

### DID YOU KNOW?

ZAHA WON TWO CAPS FOR ENGLAND UNDER ROY HODGSON, BUT THE CRYSTAL PALACE BOSS NEVER PLAYED HIM IN A COMPETITIVE MATCH!

**Club:** Crystal Palace

**Country:** Ivory Coast

**DOB:** 10/11/1992

Three Lions bosses didn't just miss a 'trick' by not convincing Wilf to turn out for England – they've missed out on a whole host of them! The winger's got one of the biggest sets of skills around, and Jurgen Klopp once said that you can't defend against him with just one player – you need two or three defenders to stop him!

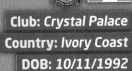

# 2
## JADON SANCHO

**TOP SKILL!**
THE CRUYFF TURN!

**DID YOU KNOW?**
HE WAS DIRECTLY INVOLVED IN MORE GOALS IN 2019-20 THAN ANY OTHER TEENAGER IN EUROPE'S TOP FIVE LEAGUES!

**Club:** Borussia Dortmund
**Country:** England
**DOB:** 25/03/2000

Imagine if Zaha WAS playing for England right now – they'd have the trickiest wingers on the planet with Sancho on the other flank too! The Three Lions youngster moves up three spaces from last year's countdown after another jaw-dropping campaign at Dortmund – he created more chances for his side than any other team-mate!

CONFIDENCE
96

DRIBBLING
96

TRICKS
96

AGILITY
95

WEAK FOOT
88

# JADON SAN

## LEAVING MAN. CITY!

**SANCHO SAYS:** "From a young age I was used to moving away from home, so that's what made me take that a step further, to leave England. I missed my mum and sisters a lot. But I want to be a professional footballer for the long term, so I had to do what I needed to do to be successful and what's best for my career."

## PLAYING ABROAD!

**SANCHO SAYS:** "Obviously I wouldn't just tell somebody to move because not everyone is comfortable moving away from home. But if you feel that you are ready to play abroad and you believe in yourself that you would do well, then I'd say, 'Why not?' I would definitely recommend it from my own experience."

# CHO

## DESCRIBING HIS STYLE!

**SANCHO SAYS:** "I'd say I'm a bit tricky, direct and obviously confident. I believe in myself in one-v-one situations. That sums me up, really! I just want to try to be the best that I can be. I want to keep working hard and never give up!"

## FAVOURITE FOOTBALLER!

**SANCHO SAYS:** "Growing up, I used to watch Ronaldinho on YouTube. That was a big thing for me. I liked how he used to carry his team sometimes with his performances. He used to try things that no one else would try and that made me like him a lot!"

## WEARING THE NO.7 SHIRT!

**SANCHO SAYS:** "I was kind of surprised when Dortmund offered Ousmane Dembele's shirt to me when I first signed, but then I realised, 'Why not?', you know? I believe in myself, so why not? Obviously I have to thank the manager for believing in me."

## LEARNING HIS GAME!

**SANCHO SAYS:** "Christian Pulisic is someone who I learnt from. His confidence in taking on players is great. 'You've just got to do your thing – that's why you're here. Make everyone understand that you're Jadon Sancho!' That's what he used to tell me!"

## WINNING THE U17 WORLD CUP!

**SANCHO SAYS:** "The England U17s were a very special group. All of us had a great bond within the team when we were in India back in 2017. We didn't know how great we were as a team, but reaching the U17 Euros final earlier that year made us realise that we had something special. We knew we could go all the way – and the team did!"

## PLAYING FOR ENGLAND!

**SANCHO SAYS:** "It means a lot to me, because when I was a young kid I always dreamed of playing for my country. It's the biggest thing that could ever happen to a young kid like me, so I am really grateful for the opportunity. I hope that I can progress with the team!"

## BRIGHT FUTURE!

**SANCHO SAYS:** "The growth in England at the moment is crazy! There are a lot of great young players out there. I'm grateful that I'm living the dream, and I hope the other young players fulfil their potential too."

# NEYMAR

**Club:** *PSG*
**Country:** *Brazil*
**DOB:** *05/02/1992*

For the third year in a row, Neymar stands on top of MATCH's top tricksters podium – and who can argue? He was told off by a referee in 2019-20 for pulling off a Rainbow Flick, because the ref thought that Ney was showboating, and attempted to pass the ball with his bum in another match – you can't get any 'cheekier' than that!

## DID YOU KNOW?
NEYMAR'S SCORED MORE CHAMPO LEAGUE GOALS THAN ANY BRAZILIAN – AND MORE THAN LEGENDS RONALDO AND RONALDINHO COMBINED!

TOP SKILL!

RAINBOW FLICK!

CONFIDENCE
98

DRIBBLING
97

TRICKS
99

AGILITY
95

WEAK FOOT
90

# STAT NEYMAR ATTACK!

NEYMAR is our gold medal winner once again, so get a load of some of the sickest stats and facts from his career!

**198**

His £198 million move to PSG in 2017 made him the world's most expensive player ever!

**3**

The highest he's ever finished in the Ballon d'Or vote is third - he won bronze in 2015 behind Leo Messi and Cristiano Ronaldo!

**72**

He was directly involved in 72 goals from his first 50 league matches for PSG. Wowzers!

**14**

Neymar spent time at Real Madrid's academy La Fabrica when he was just 14 years old, but chose to return to Brazil!

**17**

He made his professional debut when he was just 17 years old for his first club Santos!

**12**

West Ham had a £12 million bid rejected for an 18-year-old Neymar back in 2010!

## 9.9

He averaged more league dribbles per game in 2019-20 than any other star in Europe's top five leagues. Hero!

## 1

His stunning solo effort for Santos v Flamengo in 2011 won him the Puskas Award – the world's best goal of the calendar year!

## 60+

He's scored over 60 times for Brazil, and is among the top three goalscorers for his country – and the top five for matches played!

## 56,000

Around 56,000 fans turned up at the Nou Camp to see Neymar presented as a Barcelona player back in 2013 – a record for a Brazil player. Popular!

## 5

He's won five league titles since moving to Europe – two for Barca and three for PSG. Class!

# FIFA SKILLS

## SHOWBOATING — *Use these to really show off against your opponent!*

### QUICK BALL ROLLS ★★★★

This trick allows you to move the ball from one foot to the other, so a dribbler like Eden Hazard is amazing at it!

**HOLD:** R Stick Down

R ↓

PERFECT PLAYER
**EDEN HAZARD**

1

2

### ELASTICO ★★★★★

Brazil is the birthplace of this move, so it makes sense to use it with one of the Samba Stars' best-ever dribblers!

**ROTATE:** R Stick 180°
R ← ↑ →

**OR ROTATE:** R Stick 180°
R → ↑ ←

PERFECT PLAYER
**DOUGLAS COSTA**

1

2

## RAINBOW ★★★★

You can score a real screamer by using this move before hitting a volley, so use James to pull off the spectacular!

**FLICK:** R Stick Down, R Stick Up + R Stick Up

R ↓   R ↑   R ↑

**PERFECT PLAYER**
**JAMES RODRIGUEZ**

1

2

## SOMBRERO FLICK ★★★★★

Nobody makes defenders look silly more often than Neymar, and this sick move allows him to totally embarrass them!

**FLICK:** (While standing) R Stick Up, R Stick Up + R Stick Down

R ↑   R ↑   R ↓

**PERFECT PLAYER**
**NEYMAR**

1

2

# WORDSEARCH

### Find 30 jaw-dropping skill moves in the giant grid below!

```
U L E M                                                         D B K S
G R T Z                                                         N D Z R
M M G H                                                         B N S A
C V J U                                                         I O W I
U H A A                                                         P L W R
I K L R I J I G N I F E D E N M G L F F Z X W G D Y D G Y S
F H T I D B S O N G J U L H H P I W Z F F L P S W J N P R W
M T O J F C C N R B Q E B G Y J A U W P L Q C C I I O O C S
P I D L X Q X U U X W X O M G T R Q M H S U X O H S V S M
D V X F K B M L T O U Z L F J U F R Z I R T O O C S P K P C
U W T X B Y U K F K S V A K N G J Y P Z L R F L I O F K I X
N D R L H C O Q F Z D S S Y C Z M L V G F G E C H Y U C N O
W K O Q I L X S Y Q E P I O J V R G T J T E S L B A I C F V
H P G H Z B M Y U P L Z E I H S Y R G D H Z L P Q V Z G P T
X A H P F H N S R U Y B F W S B O P A A A A A V M M G W U A U
N B H C H Q I U C D A O L D S T B T O G B I P Q C Z I M R M
N U A Z V H I C K V V Y V I M B H C D N Q T K N X G B E R T U
M L T C C T A O V K O K C I L F T S E H C C W O E M P S D I
O R A H M R W P C A E D C K C B H G J A J C I T I A I N M H E
T Z I T Z P Q S J Z F B P H Y X I S C I E L Z Q D X S T L T
L P Y E R A S U E C D V T M T W M E U E U F D V Y E E A J F
H O E L V L A C O A U B C H L V L Y B H X O U Z S F S N C Q
A M P T O F Y O O F L D V T A O A L W D O R L A P T Y C T F
M I Y O Z P S H E E U G W M N W D Z E R Y E K P I X C Z A O
Q G U R G I D T F P P W I C E E I D B O M R V C N G K V Q H
V R H N U L Y S E B F V C Z C T T I K F L B O X Q E C K G N
E Y P A C F S X E P L T N I H T A I S X R M E Y U M I L F I
R D Z D O H O Z J G O T V A A E C P W Q H O O J I T L W Y P
U L L O R L L A B A N V N I N L K L E F L S R K J U F X U K
X H M W A R B B B V S O E S G U U S B V Q L J X C N L D E M
D K S I Z M O J H O B P A R E O M S O D F R I D U W H E E N U
U I Y W A A Z Z C A U G U O J R H B N W A W V Z Y J E O U K
T Y Y T O Q S W R Q H M A G A D J M B W I O X X L W H T C C
H D H O M W T R D S J Y K C I L F W O B N I A R W C J T I A
S O Q H A L N N H X V X L A D O C G V J A W N H E Q K Y T B
I Y N S H I F P I O J H J X B C U C L V E J J U A Q E H K G
P R H E H H F O T E R A Q G R N F G H L A C R O Q U E T A A
G V O K G L X H Q Z F X N S S O A O D O I B W H H S A T J R
T E A A A R O U N D T H E W O R L D O Y P H I I D U M M Y D
R H M F F A K A W A K A W H N D Q H W H F E F Z O R R T R P
```

| | | | | |
|---|---|---|---|---|
| Around The World | Cruyff Turn | Feint | La Croqueta | Roulette |
| Ball Hop | Drag Back | Flip Flap | Lane Change | Scissors |
| Ball Roll | Dummy | Heel Chop | McGeady Spin | Sombrero Flick |
| Bolasie Flick | El Tornado | Heel Flick | Nutmeg | Spin |
| Chest Flick | Elastico | Hocus Pocus | Rabona | Stepover |
| Chop | Fake Shot | Juggle | Rainbow Flick | Waka Waka |

# FOOTY MIS-MATCH

Study these snaps of legendary Milan skiller Kaka, then try to find the ten differences!

ANSWERS ON PAGE 60

# PICK YOUR TOP 5 WOMEN SKILLERS!

**DEBINHA**
North Carolina Courage & Brazil

**MARTA**
Orlando Pride & Brazil

**ROSE LAVELLE**
Man. City & USA

For the chance to win this mind-blowing gaming bundle, just write down your five favourite women skillers on the football planet, fill out your contact details and email a photograph of this page to: **match.magazine@kelsey.co.uk.** Closing date: January 31, 2021. What are you waiting for?

1.

2.

3.

4.

5.

NAME:

DATE OF BIRTH:

ADDRESS:

MOBILE:

EMAIL:

## Wordfit P20

## Eden Hazard Quiz P21

1. Older; 2. True; 3. Lille;
4. Arsenal; 5. True.

## The Nickname Game P31

1. Douglas Costa – A. Flash;
2. Kingsley Coman – D. The King;
3. Jadon Sancho – E. The Rocket;
4. Philippe Coutinho –
C. The Little Magician;
5. Stephan El Shaarawy
– B. The Pharaoh;
6. Marcus Rashford –
F. Beansprouts.

## Spot The Ball P21

H9.

## Odd One Out P31

Marcelo.

## Face In The Crowd P45

## Crossword P30

## Brain-Buster P44

1. False; 2. Chelsea; 3. Watford;
4. More than 150; 5. Barcelona;
6. Algeria; 7. 16 years old;
8. Ronaldinho; 9. More than
£50 million; 10. adidas.

## Wordsearch P56

## Footy Mis-Match P57

# SUBSCRIBE TO MATCH! & GET THIS EPIC GIFT!*

## AWESOME BOOMPODS SPEAKER WORTH £34.99!

SAVE OVER 30% ON THE SHOP PRICE!

### PACKED EVERY WEEK WITH...

★ Cool gear & quizzes     ★ Interviews & stats     ★ Megastars & more!

## HOW TO SUBSCRIBE TO MATCH!

### CALL
**01959 543 747**
QUOTE: MATAN21

### ONLINE
**SHOP.KELSEY.CO.UK/ MATAN21**